A Pictorial View
of
Old Lowton
by
H. Worsley

Best wishes to Mary & John

Dec 1st 1993

ISBN 0 9511102 2 5

A Pictorial View of Old Lowton
by H. Worsley
First Published November 1993

Published by H. Worsley
Lowton House Farm
496 Newton Road
Lowton
Warrington WA3 1PL

Designed and printed by
Willow Printing
75 - 79 Back Cross Lane
Newton-le-Willows
Merseyside WA12 9YE
Tel: (0925) 222449 / 228524

Other books by the
same author

Family Furrows
Published January 1986 (ISBN 0 951102 0 9)
2nd Edition December 1992

and

The Dwindling Furrows of Lowton
Published December 1988 (ISBN 0 9511102 1 7)

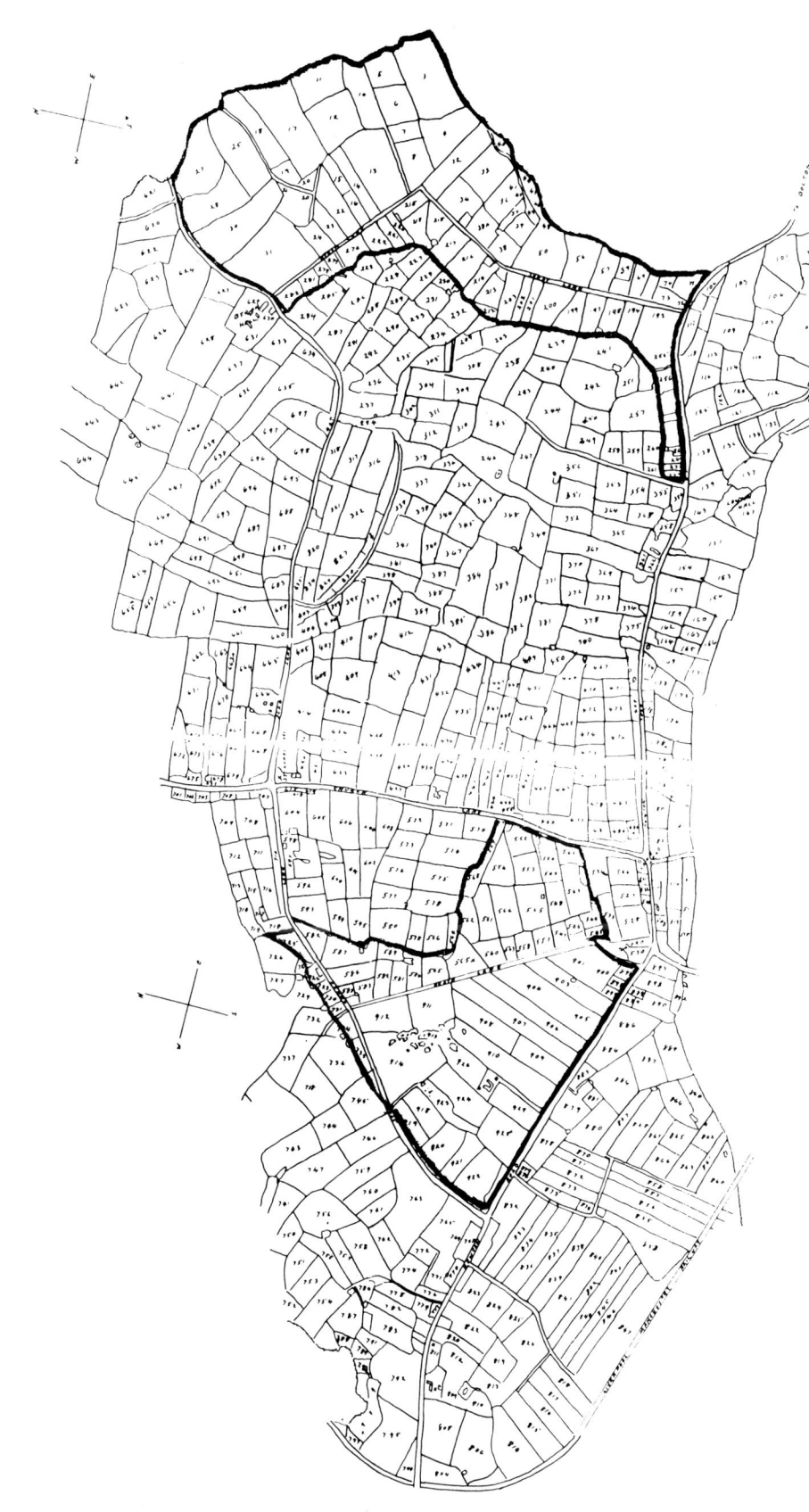

1838 Tithe Map of Lowton showing Heath and Common.

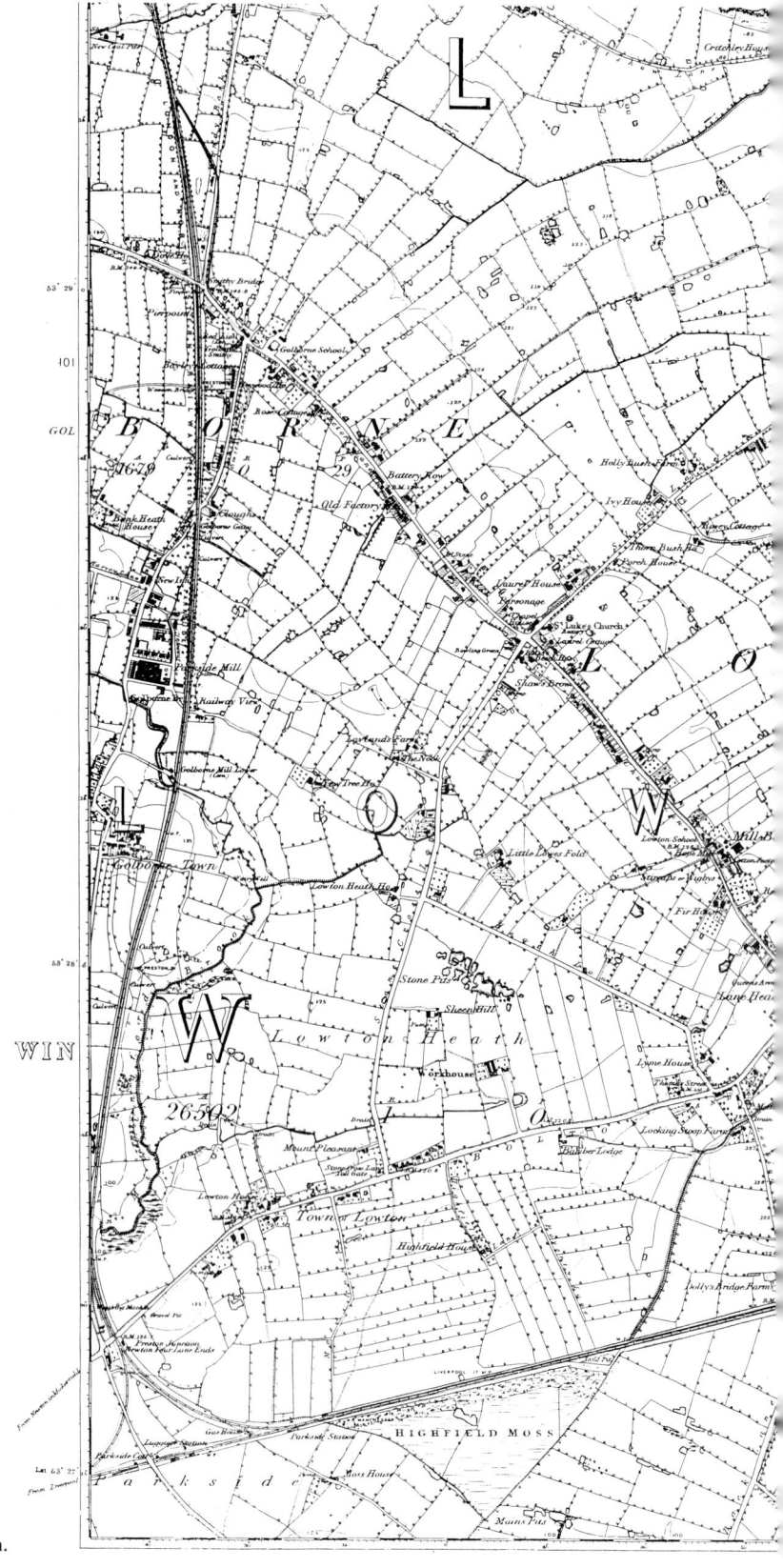

1847 Ordnance Map of Lowton.

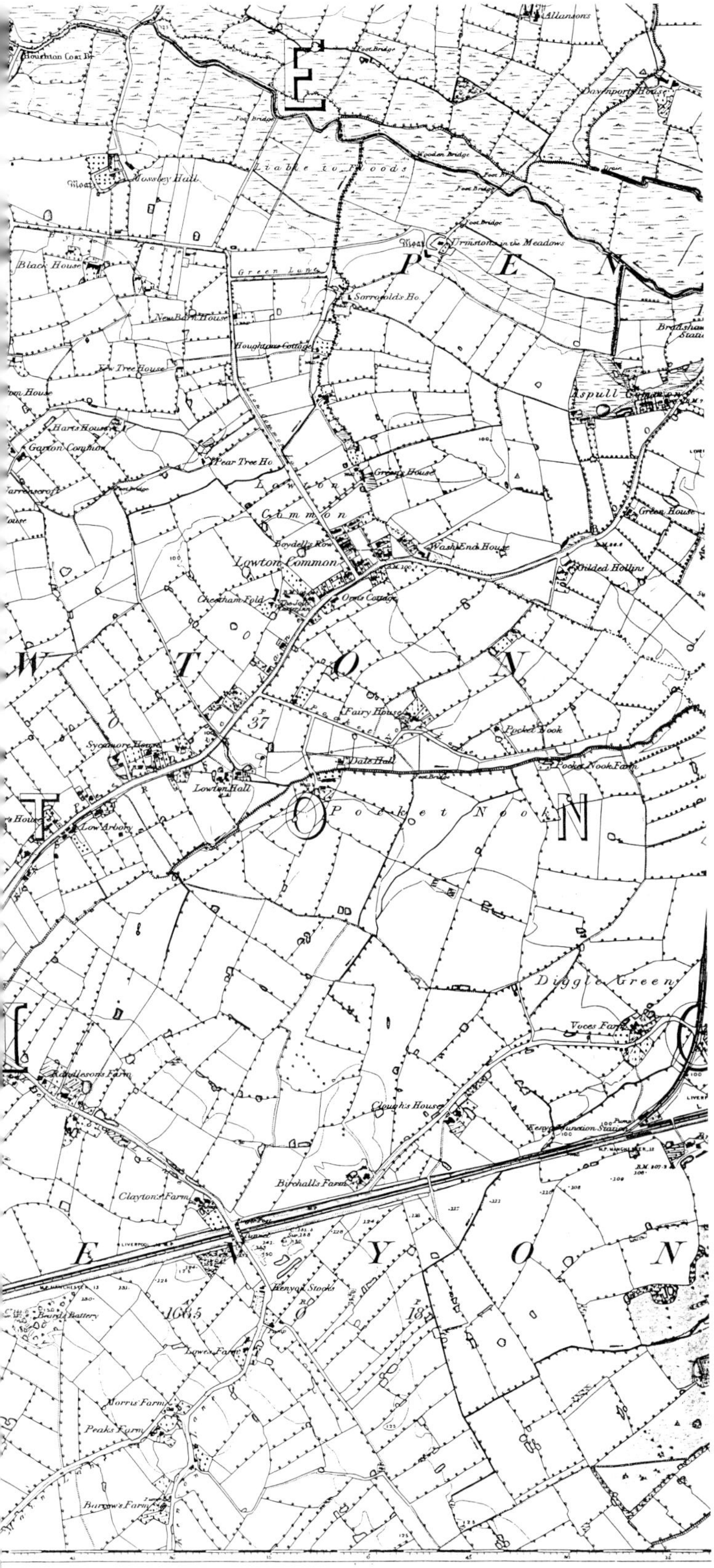
Allansons
Foot Bridge
Davenports House
Foot Bridge
Wooden Bridge
Foot Br.
Foot Bridge
Drain
Mossley Hall
Moat
Liable to Floods
Moat
Urmstons in the Meadows
Black House
Green Lane
Sorrowolds Ho.
New Barn House
Houghtons Cottage
Bradshaw
Yew Tree House
Aspull Common
Harts House
Garton Common
Pear Tree Ho
Greens House
Green House
Lowton Common
Boydells Row
Wash End House
Gilded Hollins
Cheetham Fold
Fairy House
Pocket Nook
Sycamore House
Dale Hall
Pocket Nook Farm
Lowton Hall
Low Arbory
Pocket Nook
Diggle Green
Voces Farm
Clough's House
Kenyon Junction Station
Birchalls Farm
Claytons Farm
Kenyon Stocks
Lowes Farm
Morris Farm
Peaks Farm
Barrow's Farm

Acknowledgements.

I would like to thank all those who have made their photographs available to me, and given me the information to enable me to compile this book of pictures recording some of the interesting things of the past in this old village of Lowton.

My gratitude to-
Mr. & Mrs. E. Ward, Mrs. Brennan, Mrs. Parker, Mr. J. Mort, Mr. J. Talbot, Mr. & Mrs. Kinsella, Mr. & Mrs. Twist, Mr. & Mrs. A. Wood, Mr. F. Ackers, Mr. & Mrs. Rimmington, Mr. & Mrs. Draper, Mr. & Mrs. H. Rowlinson, Mrs. B. Prescott, Mrs. A. Litherland, Mr. & Mrs. W. Adamson, Messrs H. R. & M. Howarth, Mrs. Mawdesley, Mrs. Pearson, Mrs. A. Freeman, Mr. & Mrs. Vaudrey, Mr. J. Maconie, Mr. H. Smith, Miss. D. Collier, Mr. A. R. Thompson, Mr. & Mrs. A. Hughes, Mr. & Mrs. J. Gaskell, Mrs. B. Nicholls, Mr. & Mrs. E. Bishop, Mr. & Mrs. R. Marsh, Dr. & Mrs. Fairhurst and Lancashire County Cricket Club.

Thanks also to Mr. J. Farrington for granting me permission to use three photographs of St. Lukes School classes, and to Wigan Record Office Archives for permission to print several of their photographs.

Particular thanks to Mr. A. Soper for allowing me to use his paintings.

My appreciation to Mr. Tony Ashcroft of the Heritage Services, and to Mr. Len Hudson of the Archive Services for the help they gave me during my research.

H. Worsley

Introduction

During the writing of my books about the village of Lowton many photographs were made available to me, since that time I have collected quite a few more and feel they ought to be published so that people might remember something of the fast disappearing village and try to picture how it was even as recently as seventy years ago before the East Lancashire Road cut through, making a north-south divide.

For centuries there had been another kind of division, there was the Heath in the west and the Common in the east, even today some of my generation refer to these districts as Th'eath and Th'commmon. To define the extent of the Heath and the Common at the time of the Enclosure Award for Lowton in 1766 I placed the plan of the enclosures on the 1838 tithe map, the new field boundaries fitted exactly to the old. The Heath and Common at that time covered an area of 180 acres. The tithe map with the Heath and the Common clearly marked are on another page, as is the 1847 ordnance map of Lowton.

Until recent times Lowton seems to have been a village of small isolated communities which were known to everyone by its particular name,- Iron Fold, Lowes Fold, Rookery Fold, Cheetham Fold, Penkethman Fold, Saddle Tree Fold, Belle Vue, Warrens Croft, The Grove, The Nook, Mount Taber, Th'Hammer Street, Waterside, Barracks, Canaan and Pocket Nook. Lowton was also an independent village with no large land owner, the tithe schedule shows there were more than a hundred small land owners including upwards of seventy farms and small holdings. Many have disappeared altogether, others altered beyond recognition, with no one having a photograph to show what they were like, hopefully this collection will preserve some of the old scenes.

Originally Lowton was in the parish of Winwick, in 1732 a Chapel of Ease was built at the junction of Stone Cross Lane and the Head Lane as it was called, to save the people of Lowton and Golborne the long walk to Winwick Church. In 1845 St Lukes Parish was formed and in 1860 Lowton was divided into two parishes, St Mary's being built at Lowton Common.

I have attempted to place the pictures in a reasonable kind of sequence but any that had been overlooked or came late for printing may be towards the end of the book. Not all the photographs were good to copy and I apologise if the quality of a number of them is poor. I am deeply grateful to Mr. A. Soper for allowing me to use his paintings were photographs were not available to me.

It is a great pity from the historians point of view that many of the old properties have been modernised, and in some cases altered so much that they bear little resemblance to the original buildings.

H. Worsley.

Above- St. Lukes Church.

Erected in 1732 as a Chapel of Ease when Lowton was still in the Parish of Winwick, it was reputedly built on the site of an old stone cross, on land given by Hugh Stirrup. Painting by A. Soper.

Below:-
St. Lukes became a parish in 1845 the Rev. John Pennington being the first rector. The tower was added in 1860. Picture about 1920.

Photo courtesy of Wigan M.B.C.

Left-
Interior of St. Lukes before modernisation, note the box pews.

Below:-
The name plates from many of the pews have been preserved by mounting them on a display board and can be seen in the chancel. The right to sit in the pew could be bought, sold or left in a will as in that of John Worsley 28th October 1757.
"Wife Mary to have the room called the parlour to live in in Lowton House during her life, with the cellar and the little buttery, and the liberty of sitting in the pew."

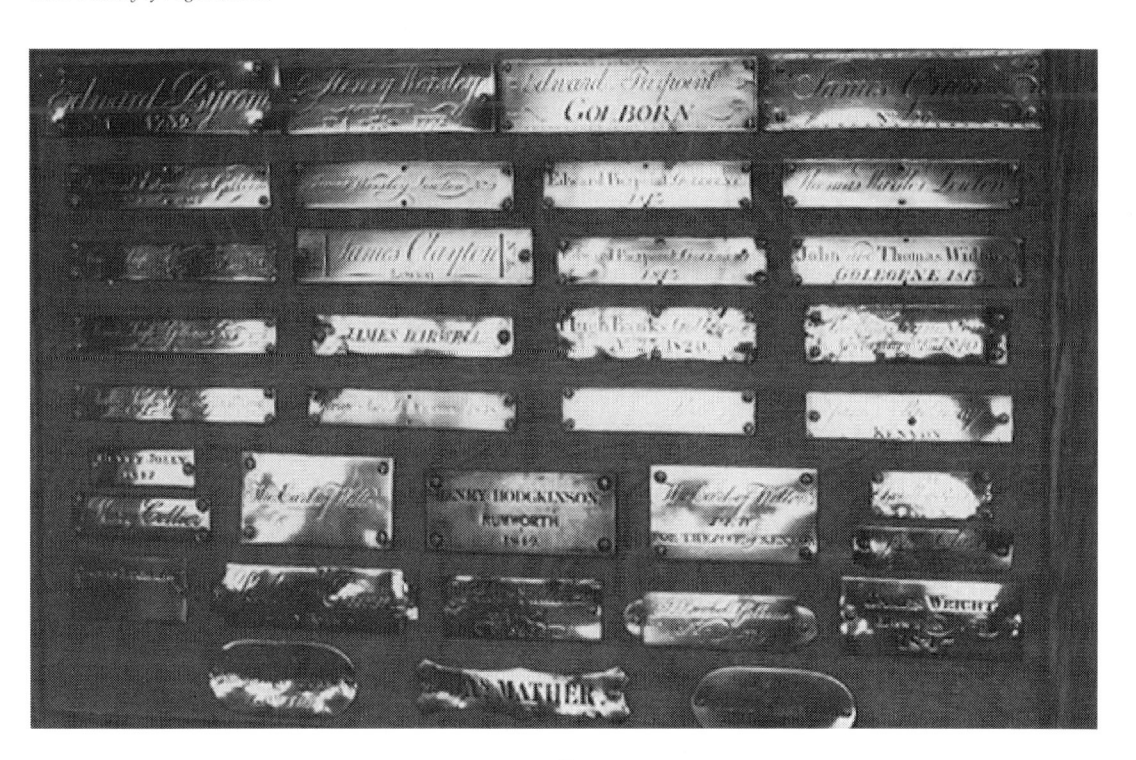

Photo courtesy of Wigan M.B.C.

Photo courtesy of Wigan M.B.C.

Above-
Cottages demolished to extend grave yard of St. Lukes.

Below:-
The same cottages showing the barn at Manor Farm in the back ground.

Photo courtesy of Wigan M.B.C.

Left:-
Church Walking Day in the 1930's. Procession in Stone Cross Lane approaching the Nook led by P.C. Edmonson.

In those early days the procession was led by a brass band, it proceeded to Lowton House the home of Mr. James Glover C.C. J.P. who was also the lay reader at St. Lukes, there the children were given sweets and an orange before returning via Newton Road to Lane Head and Church Lane.

Left-
St. Lukes Church Sunday morning 28th January 1940.

Left-
A Church outing in the 1920's.

11

Right-
The Old Rectory in Golborne Road.

Below-
A school was first opened in 1751, brought into being by money from the sale of land owned by six benefactors the principal being the Lord of the Manor.

Previously Scholars were housed in various places - The Old Rectory, a house in Stone Cross Lane, another in Church Lane, and one in Newton Road in the Lane Head area.

Right-
The second school built in 1870, originally for a boys school, but after a very short period became a mixed school. It is still in use today.

Left- Church Lane.

In the foreground on the left is the "Little School", while the second farthest gable is the old school house with the "Big School" standing some twenty yards back.

Beyond the farthest gable and perhaps thirty yards from the road stood the cotton mill, then known as the Victoria mill. It was burned down early in the century and taken over about 1920 by William Hindley who founded the Sovereign Toffee Works.

The row of houses in the distance was called "The Iron Fold".

Above- Beech House.

Built by a silk mercer in the first half of the nineteenth century when silk weaving was the main cottage industry in the village.

Above-

Manor House Farm, Church Lane.

Above-
Golborne Road during the laying of the sewer in 1938, centre of the picture is the old rectory, at the end of the distant row of houses is Jesse Mort's shop.

Below-
Looking the other way is Church Lane with Manor House Farm on the left and Beech House behind trees on the right.

Above-
Ashwood Farm, Church Lane. Farmed for many years by the Talbots and latterly by Farringtons for 50 years. Built 1715.

Below-
Stirrups Farm is in a dilapidated condition once owned by the family who gave the land on which St. Lukes Church was built. Stands about 200 yards off Church Lane in the fields opposite St. Lukes day school.

Above-
Looking down Church Lane from Lane Head before the East Lancashire Road was built about 1928 showing some of the "Waterside" houses and the two rows of terraced houses, the "New Road" eventually passed between them. The wagon is from the Sovereign Confectionery Co.

Below-
Two pictures of the houses that stood on the right of Church Lane which were demolished to make way for the road. Jack Worsley the taxi proprietor lived there, his picture is on another page.

16

Above-
Aerial view of Sovereign Confectionery Works in the fore ground the cottages called Iron Fold, on the left the school and school house.

Below-
Church Lane looking from where the East Lancashire Road crosses the lane.

Above-
Sovereign Transport Department - Part of the fleet of wagons with capacities from 3-15 tons. Mr. Walter Ball the transport manager is on the extreme right.

Below-
Section of caramel boiling department.

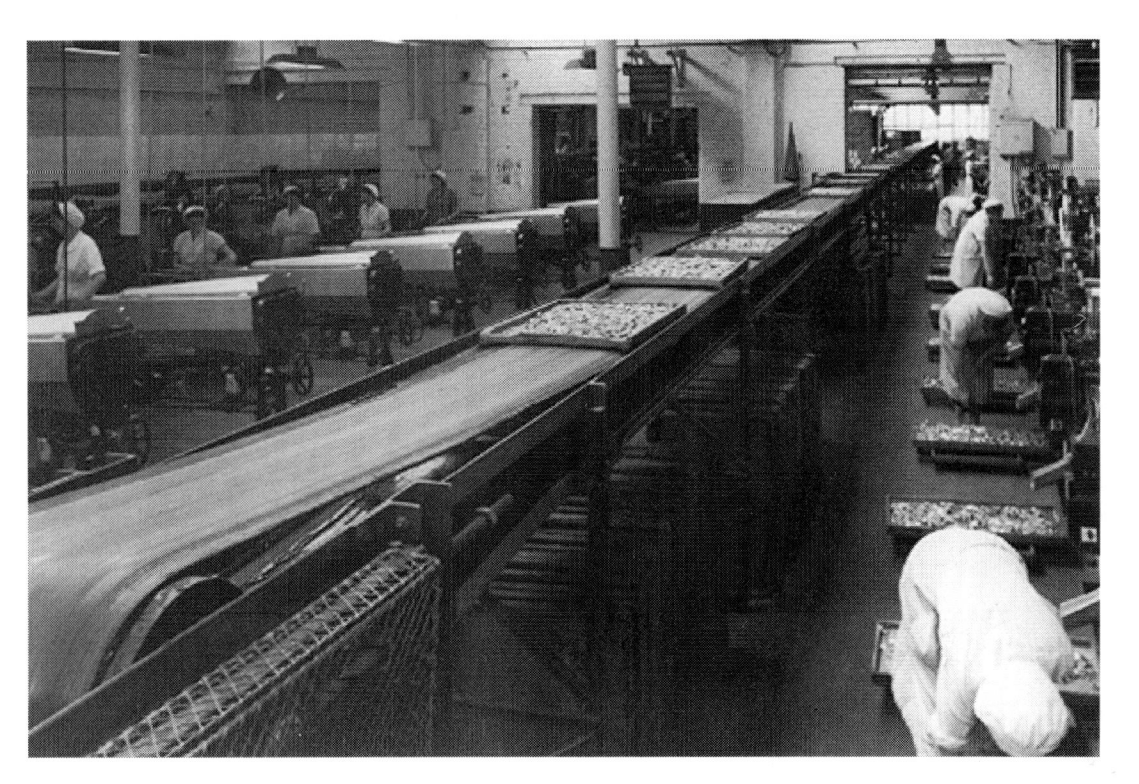

Above-
High speed cut and wrap machines with an output of 750 wrapped caramels each machine per minute.

Below-
High speed machines used exclusively in the manufacture of creamy whirls.

Above-
Packaging Department - Automatic weighing and cartoning.

Below-
Loading Bay - with goods for Ethiopia in the foreground.

Left-
East wing of Sandfield Hall close by the old Lowton Junction station. When George V stayed in the siding near by he spent the evenings at the hall.

Built at the end of last century by Aireys the brewers of Wigan.

Right-
Lowton Station right on the western boundary of the village, supposed to have been one of the best kept stations in the north, possibly because of the Royal visits.

From painting by A. Soper.

Left-
George V and Queen Mary arriving, note the limousines waiting on the bridge.
Date around 1928.

Right-
Sand Up Farm one of Lord Newton's farms. Tenanted by the Boydells for many years.

Above-
Recently known as Barlows Cottages were silk weavers cottages demolished about 1960.

Right-
Banks Farm, was owned until 1918 by Earl Wilton and farmed by the Banks family for more than a century.

Above-
Marsh House built about 1900 on the site of the old Cross Keys Inn. The date stone of 1703 is from the old house.

Left- Lowton House
Once the home of Robert Houghton who bought the toll gates from Stone Cross Lane and erected them at Holly House and Lowton House Farm. Later his son-in-law Mr James Glover J.P. owned the properties until his death in 1944. The small estate of Lowton Gardens now occupy the site.

Right-
Old cottages belonged to the small estate of Lowton House. They were across the road from Lowton Gardens.

Left-
From a painting by A. Soper. Lowton House Farm as it was at the beginning of the century. The deeds go back before 1700. Note the Toll Bar Gates.

Right-
Mr. William Balshaw a tenant from 1902 until 1934.

Left-
Coach House and stables at Lowton House. The saddle room was used as a Sunday school for the children at this end of the village. Mr. Glover's daughter took the class in the upstairs room with the window in the Gable end.

Left-
Wilton Cottage a small holding once belonging to the estate of Earl Wilton. It stands perilously by the edge of Newton Road.

Left-
Lowton Cottage said to have been built by a Liverpool merchant probably before 1800. A lean-to had been added to the back as a silk weaving room.

Above- Holly House
A perfect example of a late Georgian country house built around 1800.

Right-
A view of the back of the house showing the window design much favoured at that period.

Left-
Looking west along Newton Road from the Travellers Rest. On the left is the gable end of the outbuildings to Wilton Cottage, on the right stands Byroms Farm, in the distance are the very ornate railings of Lowton House.

Left-
The rear of Byroms Farm, note the heavy flagged roof, small paned windows and some unusual design in the brick work.

Like Lowton House Farm would have been built in the 1600's. From 1800 until 1868 farmed by the Bridges. Three generations of Bents farmed there for the next 98 years.

Above-
Newton Road looking east from Lowton House showing Byroms Farm and the giant chestnut that dominated this part of the village.

Right-
The well at Byroms Farm, it is still useable and situated only 10 yards from the road.

Right-
The well preserved milestone opposite Lowton Cottage possibly been there since the main road was rebuilt in 1765. There is a second one at Lane Head and a third by St. Marys Church wall.

Above- Picture taken about 1900 of the compilers uncle and great-grandfather, James and Richard Ashton, Richard was a prize gooseberry grower. The cottage stood on what is now the Travellers Rest car park.

Below- The Travellers Rest about the same period, the two white cottages are now part of the inn. In the farther one lived Michael Garrity a well know local character. In 1870 the cottages beyond were used as a school by the landlords daughters called the Miss Mayhews.

Right-
Dunkirk Hall demolished 1950's reputed at the time to be the oldest house in Lowton.

Situated on Newton Road next to the corner shop, once the old toll house.

In the back are the cottages known as Mount Pleasant.

Right-
The old shop window in 1928.

Right-
The old Toll House for Stone Cross Lane standing next to Dunkirk Hall. The road was tolled in 1829 and the toll house replaced an older building in 1854. Tolls were ended about 1880 when it became a dwelling house and shop. In the distance can be seen the row of old cottages locally called Th'ackey or the Moss View.

Picture taken 1934.

Left-
Picturesque Snowdrop Cottage on the corner of Stone Cross Lane and Newton Road. In the early days of the century Mr. William Hill's garden was admired by all the passers by.

Above-
This row of old cottages was always known as Th'ackey or Th'Moss View. In the 1920's Mr Maudsley had a cycle shop, he also ran a taxi and sold paraffin and petrol. Later he was first to install a petrol pump. He is seen here assisting a motorist. Behind the houses were two more cottages, one was unoccupied and used as a bandroom by the local brass band. Most of the cottages had long rooms for silk weaving.

Mr John Ashton organist at the Primitive Methodist chapel for almost 50 years also conducted and ran the brass band for many years until the out break of the 1914 war.

Because the members were Methodists and abstainers they were known locally as Th'Buttermilk Band.

Above-
Croft Cottage sometimes known as Pear Tree 434 Newton Road was for many years occupied by Mr. James Hodson pictured here with his daughter and grand-daughter.. He was a stalwart member of the Primitive Methodist Chapel, it was said he never missed a service or a Sunday School session for over 60 years. He was presented with a medallion which his family still treasure today.

Below-
Brook Cottage once a small holding with out buildings both are typical weavers cottages.

Right- Round House
No one knows the reason why it was so called, it was completely square. Thought at one time to be a toll office but there is no proof. In the 1840's when there was trouble in the cottage silk weaving industry news bulletins were issued, many could not read so they gathered in groups to hear one of their number read it to them, a man named Adamson was reputed to have used the round house for this purpose.

Below-
An artists impression of "Mount Tabor" built in 1817 as a Parish Poor House, known locally as "Thowd Work - Heause" but in 1850 the poor were transferred to Leigh, and alterations made to create eleven cottages. Most of the early tenants were Methodists belonging to the Chapel at Winwick Lane, and it was said that one of them whose turn it was to entertain the preacher for the day did not like the name of Work house and said so to the gentleman, he suggested a biblical name might be more appropriate, "Why not call it "Mount Tabor", then I would feel among brethren." The houses were demolished in 1939. The site is about 200 yards north of Newton Road, and the lane leading to it is approximately 400 yards east of the junction with Stone Cross Lane.

Left-
Highfield Farm 300 yards south of Newton Road. It is not known when it was built but it is marked on Yates Ordnance Map of 1786.

Note the lean-to weaving shed. When I was a boy there were still one or two silk shuttles in that work room.

Left:-
The lane leading from Highfield Farm to Newton Road with Croft Cottage and Brook Cottage in the background.

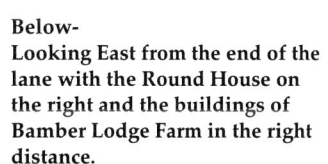

Below-
Looking East from the end of the lane with the Round House on the right and the buildings of Bamber Lodge Farm in the right distance.

Above-
Greens Farm or Bamber Lodge, a typical nineteenth century farm yard with Adamsons the farmers and friend Mr. Ball.

Below-
This old cottage was demolished more than twenty years ago. No.345 Newton Road was built on the site. Originally there was an old barn and several acres of glebe land.

A Visit From The Past

It is incredible how the human mind hears what it expects to hear, for example a birds call in the garden that mimics a far off telephone and makes one rush to a non-ringing telephone.

Despite being married for some six years my wife and I had not been blessed with any children and as a couple we had thought it worthwhile to foster new born babies prior to their adoption and as a result of that decision we had acted as foster parents for some extremely young babies who had been as young as six days old.

One baby called John brought with him a totally different phenomena into our home. I had often heard him crying in the nursery which was the smallest bedroom on the first floor, when apparently he was not even in it and even our old labrador would stop and look up the stairs listening to the sound which was emanating from this particular bedroom. This all came to a head one Thursday afternoon when my wife went to the local supermarket. The baby started crying quite loudly and I must admit to being somewhat annoyed with being left with the baby when there was a possibility that I might have to go out on call. I went up the stairs to the bedroom but as soon as my hand touched the bedroom door the crying stopped and upon opening the door I found the cot was empty.

That night I rather sheepishly explained what I had been hearing, even to describing the sobbing type of cry and was amazed and relieved to learn that my wife had been hearing a similar phenomena also, in fact she heard it even earlier than me, in that she first heard this crying shortly after receiving the telephone request to accept this particular baby.

The crying continued to occur the whole time that John stayed with us and I must admit rather hesitantly that I had slept with the light on whenever I slept alone in the cottage. It is a peculiar feeling to hear the sound of loud crying coming from a room that you know is empty particularly if you are an avowed sceptic on such matters. The crying stopped as soon as John left us and has not reoccurred. Enquiries about previous such episodes in the cottage had drawn a blank.

However our cleaner who new nothing of our experiences did on a separate occasion see a shadow of a woman with a distressed baby in her arms at the top of the stairs outside of this particular bedroom; the cleaner did on that occasion leave the cottage rather hastily.

Dr. G. J. Fairhurst

Above-
Rose Cottage Newton Road, the date of 1695 is carved on one of the beams of this lovely old cottage.

Dr. Fairhurst is the present owner. His remarkable story is on the previous page.

Right-
A back view of the cottage showing the long window to the weaving room.

Left-
Ormstons ran a bakery and shop from these premises at the beginning of the century.

Left-
Step Houses and Primitive Methodist Chapel before the roadway was raised. Highfield Farm can be seen on the far horizon. The Step Houses were back to back houses and on the other side the passage way was called "Th' Hammer Street".

Below-
Another view of the Step Houses

Right-
The first Primitive Methodist Chapel built in 1842 on Winwick Lane. At the time the railway was being constructed 1828 services were being held in the open air or in one of the nearby cottages until they had raised enough money to build.

Right-
In 1880 this larger Chapel was built to accomodate the growing congregation and the original Chapel was used as the Sunday school, it can be seen at the end of the row of cottages.

Right-
Chapel demolished 1985. Picture taken at a later date when a new Sunday school had been built on Newton Road and the old one sold to the council for a storage depot.

Above-
Wedding party in front of the old Chapel, at this time the Sunday school, the date would be about 1908. The gentlemen in the bowler hat is John Ashton the organist.

Below-
Another view of Winwick Lane in the early 1920's.

Right-
Interior of the Chapel before the new organ was installed in 1931.

Right-
New Sunday school built in 1913 is now a dual purpose building for Chapel and Sunday school.

Right-
Th' owd Thatch about 1890 picturing Mr. Simon Howarth a relation of the blacksmith at Lane Head. He was a Primitive Methodist lay preacher.

Aerial View of Lane Head 1960

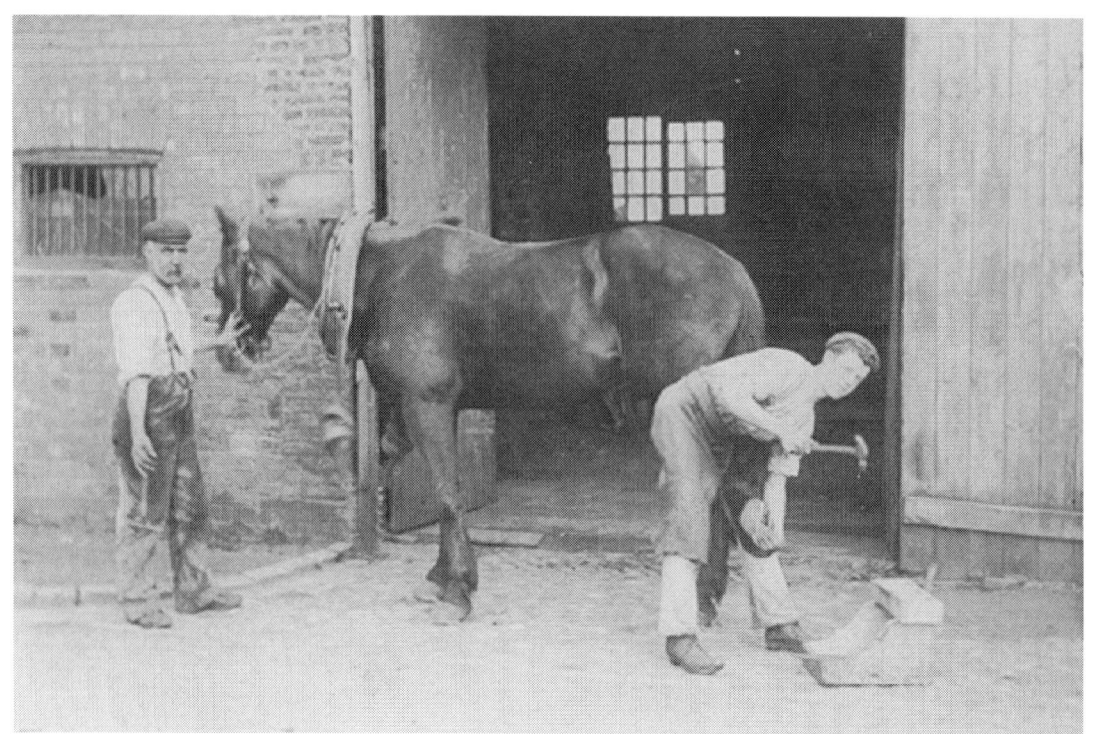

Above-
There were two smithies at Lane Head until 1920, the one above was demolished to make way for the bungalow 263 Newton Road. Jethro Higson the blacksmith keeps a watchful eye on his young apprentice, Mat Howarth, who later took over the business.
Below-
The smithy on Kenyon Lane only recently closed down. In the picture Mr. Henry Clayton waits with his grand daughters for his horse to be shod. Amos Henshaw the blacksmith and his men see to the job in hand.

Left-
For many years Mr. Judson was the post master at Lane Head.

Groceries and even poultry food could be obtained from the shop

It is now a Newsagents.

Left-
Policeman on point duty at Lane Head. The taxi is almost sure to be one of Jack Worsley's.

Left-
Lane Head and Kenyon Lane in the 1920's. The smithy in the foreground has only recently closed down. Mr. Chris Jordan followed by his son had been the blacksmith since the 1914-18 war.

The building far left was Hursts toffee works. They were famous for their "Lung - tips".

Above-
A load of cotton on fire at Lane Head in the 1920's. Most of the raw cotton for the mills in the Leigh, Bolton and Bury area was carried along Newton Road, the solid tyres of the vehicles causing havoc with the road surface.

Below-
A charabanc rally about the same period. In the distance can be seen the old cottages which were demolished when the East Lancashire Road was built.

Photo courtesy of Wigan M.B.C

Above-
Nest Farm on the Kenyon Boundary at Lane Head.

Below-
Old Cottages of Newton Road near Winwick Lane . It is said Primitive Methodist meetings were held here in the early 1800's.

Above -The Old Red Lion.
Painting by A. Soper from an old photograph. Replaced at the turn of the century by the building below.

Below-
The New Red Lion, quite famous for it's bowling green where many important matches were played. In the old days the stable yard was used as a stud. The stallions of both heavy and Vanner type horses called at regular intervals.

Left-
The Kings Arms is another Inn that was rebuilt towards the end of the century. It was formerly the Queens Arms as shown on a map of 1847 and again on the 1881 census.

Left and below-
The Cottages and shop on the left were also an inn sometimes called the White Horse. There is still one of the stained glass windows by the porch in the bottom picture. Two more are preserved by the front door of 263 Newton Road incorporated when the wheelwrights Hampsons built the bungalow on the site of the old smithy.

Right-
Howarths shop at Lane Head in the 1950's looking much the same as it did before the 1914-18 war.

Below-
The interior of the small well - stocked shop. Now Cost Cutters.

Above- Lowton Grange.
Built about 1890 on the site of a previous large house in 8 acres of woodland on Stone Cross Lane, by Mc Corquodales the printers for their son's wedding present. The sons fiancee refused to come saying "The place is not as big as my fathers stables". Eventually it was owned by Richard Clegg a cotton mill owner, followed by George Shaw the brewer, and by Major Hart of Bickershaw Collieries. The last owner was John Boardman the solicitor. The house was demolished in 1957 the site is now occupied by Grange Close.

Below-
In the happy days before the 1914 war. Mrs Clegg and friends with daughter Nora on the pony. Miss Nora Clegg was presented at court in 1920.

Right-
Grange Farm originally called The Mountains. There are the ruins of two old cottages in the yard with clay floors, they were silk weavers cottages and it was said the families lived upstairs and had their looms on the ground floor. Bents family have farmed there for more than 50 years.

Right-
The cottages at Mount Pleasant on Stone Cross Lane. Built in 1804.

There was a nursery of about 3 acres.

Right- Heath Farm.
The Boydells have farmed the land since 1880. Mr. Peter Boydell carved his name and date on one of the beams in the barn in 1880.

Above- Holly Bank.
A small holding on Heath Lane built sometime after the lane was cut through the heath during the enclosures of 1766.

Below- Thompsons Farm.
This 17th Century farm was built right on the edge of the Heath. The beams are all from ships timbers.

Above- Lime House.
Built in 1903 by William Eckersley a cotton manufacturer on the site of a former large property. Made famous locally by Mr. Eckersley's son, P.T. Eckersley who captained Lancashire CC 1929-35.
Originally the front drive was on Heath Lane.

Below-
Heath Lane in the 1920's.

Left-
Hawthorn Cottage, Stone Cross Lane opposite Nook Lane.

Painting by A Soper

Left- Shaws Brow.
The cottages had no back doors. The toilets were across the passageway at the front.

Painting by A. Soper.

Left-
Shaw's Brow Farm.
Modernised 18th Century House originally a small holding. Later a nursery.

Above-
The top of Stone Cross Lane when the sewer was laid 1939-40. The Hare and Hounds on the left, The Rams Head and cottage beyond. Who is the young boy?

Below-
Denney's Farm and Clares shop.
From a painting by A. Soper.

Above-
The Rams Head built in 1731, one year before the Church. In the early days the Parish overseers held their meetings there. Said to be the first public house in Lowton to be licensed.

Below-
The Hare and Hounds was a calling place for the Croft and Risley farmers on their way to Wigan market with their produce. As late as the 1920's the flagstone floors of the inn were stoned each day and spread with fresh sawdust.

Photo courtesy of Wigan M.B.C.

Above-
Laurel House a little way down Slag Lane from the church was quite large with some out buildings and a barn. It would seem that at one time fustian weaving and perhaps later silk weaving had been going on in one of the buildings, because within living memory there had been a small steam engine there, presumably to drive several looms. Painting by A. Soper.

Below-
Looking back along Slag Lane towards the church can be seen the substantial barn and buildings beyond belonging to Laurel House 1940.

Above-
In 1940 there were only five small farms and three or four cottages on Slag Lane, apart from the few houses on Merchants Square. This was the scene looking from Laurel House. The lane leading to the Grove was on the right opposite the farm in this picture.

Left-
Grove House a very old property.

Left-
Thorn Bush Farm now surrounded by a large estate. Further down the lane were Seddons Farm and Grove Farm.

Right-
Merchants Square locally called The Barracks.

Painting by A. Soper.

Right-
Warrens Croft Farm.
There were two or three very old properties in this little area of Warrens Croft.

Right-
Little Byrom.
A smallholding near to Byrom Hall.

Photo courtesy of Wigan M.B.C.

Above-
Byrom Hall once surrounded by a moat. The estate of Byrom existed in the Thirteenth Century and is mentioned in the Victoria History of the County of Lancashire.

Below-
Mossley Hall off Byrom Lane, built on the site of a much older property. There is still evidence of that building and the surrounding moat, both of which are shown on Yates map of 1786.

Above-
Sorrocolds Farm, off Green Lane now replaced by a modern bungalow.
Painting by A.Soper.

Below-Looking across the Flash from Sorrocolds Farm.
This part of the Pennington Flash is within the Lowton boundary. Houghton Coat bridge is in the distance near to where the Plank Lane Brook entres the Flash.

Above-
Saddle Tree Fold, now modernised, was another of the small communities. A short distance away was yet another called Belle Vue.

Below-
Elm Farm one of the sixty or more farms and small holdings of the last century.

Above-St. Catherine of Siena.
It was not until 1959 that the Roman Catholics built their church at Lane Head, before that date the people of that faith attended Church and school in either Golborne or Leigh. St. Catherines is now a thriving Church attracting many members of the new community as well as the old Lowton families.

Below-
Old Roman Catholic Church at Golborne (1920's).

Above-The Hollies.
A small holding built in the mid 1700's, Newton Road near the East Lancashire Road.

Below-Modernised Weavers Cottages Newton Road.
The one on the left also sold lengths of silk and other products such as scarves etc. At the beginning of the century the cottage on the right was the home of Mr. Page the Venetian blind maker.

Above-
Mather Lane Farm built in the 1700's home to the Drapers for all this century. For many years they ran a coal bagging business as well as farming.

Below-Charity Farm.
Once a small holding on Newton Road.

Left-
Hampsons Farm Newton Road farmed by four generations of the Howarth Family since 1800. Matthew Howarth of the third generation was also the blacksmith at Lane Head.

Left- Arbory Farm, Newton Road. Farmed in the 1800's by Mr. William Phillips.

Left-
Mr. & Mrs. Phillips and daughter Sarah Ann in 1880.

Above-
Aerial view of the coal board offices in the 1960's. See Arbory Farm in the bottom right hand corner.

Below-
Coal Board Offices, Anderton House, demolished several years ago.

Above-
Newton Road in 1940 during the laying of the sewer.

Left-
Elm Tree Cottage was a small dairy farm when the picture was taken about 1890.

Lowton Common.

From the earliest times most of the population of the village seems to have been concentrated round the Common Lane area, or Sandy Lane as it is now called, possibly because the common was more productive than the heath, the heavier land providing better pasturage than the drier soil of the heath, the worth of the land being reflected in the rents charged at the time of the enclosure. Two shillings an acre for land on the common, and one shilling an acre for land on the heath.

Many of the cottages built in the Eighteenth and early Nineteenth Century were especially made to accomondate weaving looms, some with one "shop" some with two. There were three rows of such cottages off Sandy Lane namely, Ince's Row, Hayes' Row and Gregory' Row. Gregorys also had a small factory weaving shed at the end of their row. Many of the houses along that stretch of Newton Road were weavers cottages, quite a number also had buildings attached to the houses where farm animals were kept, in fact many were small holdings with an acre or two of land.

A few of the farm houses have date stones and other evidence to show that they were built on the common before the enclosures of 1765.

The common can claim to be a little part of our countries history. In late November 1642 the battle of Lowton Common took place, the Parliamentarians in the Leigh area received word that the Royalists were coming from the north to subdue them, they quickly gathered about 3,000 horses and foot men and encountered the Royalists at Chowbent so successful were they that they drove them back through Leigh as far as Lowton Common. As for the battle I will quote from "The Civil War in Leigh and Makerfield" by Norma Ackers.

"And so we over-rode our Foote being carried with a fervent desire to overtake them, and to doe some notable service upon them, so that we drove them to Loaton common, where they, knowing our Foote to be far behind, turned faces about, and began to make head against us. Whereupon a sharpe although a short Incounter, but when they perceived our full and settled resolution, they made away as fast as their horses could carry them, and we after them, killing, wounding and taking prisoners about 200 of them, and we lost never a man ; only we had three of our men wounded, but not mortally, so that I think that they will trouble us no more out of that part of the Countrey".

Left- St.Marys Church Lowton. The parish was formed in 1860 and the Church built on land given by William J. Leigh one time M.P. for south Lancashire. Miss Leigh of Hale, Liverpool offered to be the patroness. The first vicar was Rev. J.W.S. Simpson who held the living for thirty years.

Below- St. Marys School. There is a stone in front of the school with the inscription - 'These Schools were erected by Mary Leigh of Hale, Patroness of St.Marys Church, on land given by William J. Leigh, M.P. South Lancashire. 1862'.

It is to be noted that the inscription on Lowton St. Lukes School reads - 'Erected by Mary Leigh 1854'.

Above-
St. Marys Vicarage.

Below-
Green Lawns on the corner of Newton Road and Hesketh Meadow Lane. Mentioned with affection in Richard Ridyards "Memories of Lowton".

Left-
Silk weavers cottages in Hesketh Meadow Lane.

Below left-
Another view of the cottage about which Richard Ridyard writes. Another well known Lowton weaver employed by Mr. Hilton was Rachel Smith, who died in 1927, aged 91.

"This lady lived and wove for the greater part of her life in the first of the two cottages still standing in Hesketh Meadow Lane". (Memories of Lowton 1935.)

Below-
The pink cottage, now 167 Newton Road, where Mrs. Marsh produced the last piece of silk to be woven in Lowton in 1910. Her loom and accessories were at one time in the Pennington Hall Museum. It is not known where they are today.

The cottage was demolished in 1951.

Above- Oaklands.
Built at the turn of the century by Mr John Green who started the glue works in Carr Lane in 1868. A feature in the house is the stain glass window in memory of one of his family.

It is the largest house in Lowton.

Below- The Elms.
Mr Charles Guest occupied this house for many years.

Above-
Newton Road in 1940. The car is parked by the village club.

Below-
St. Marys Station Bridge. The tram terminus was on the bridge.

Above- Cheetham Fold Farm.
Made famous by the murder of the farmer Joshua Rigby on 18th September 1883. The case was never solved and no convictions were made. The inquest took place in the Jolly Carter.

Painting by A. Soper.

Below- The Jolly Carter.
An old coaching inn thought to be at least sixteenth century.

Photo courtesy of Wigan M.B.C.

Above- Lowton Independent Methodist Church.
Built on or near the site of three former Chapels. The first building was opened by the Wesleyan Methodists in 1794, eventually to be taken over by the Independents. It was pulled down and another Chapel built in 1834. In 1849 it was necessary to build larger premises. The cause prospered so much that the present larger Chapel was opened in 1880. The Sunday School at the rear was also used as a day school.

Below-
Chapel Walk in the early days of the century.

Above-
Very old thatched cottage by St. Marys Church, burned down soon after 1900. The Wood family pictured here ran a green-grocery business from the premisies, the children delivering fruit and vegetables in large baskets.

Below-
Trams were still running in Lowton in the early 1930's, the picture shows two trams passing on a loop near the Chapel gate and the old cottage.

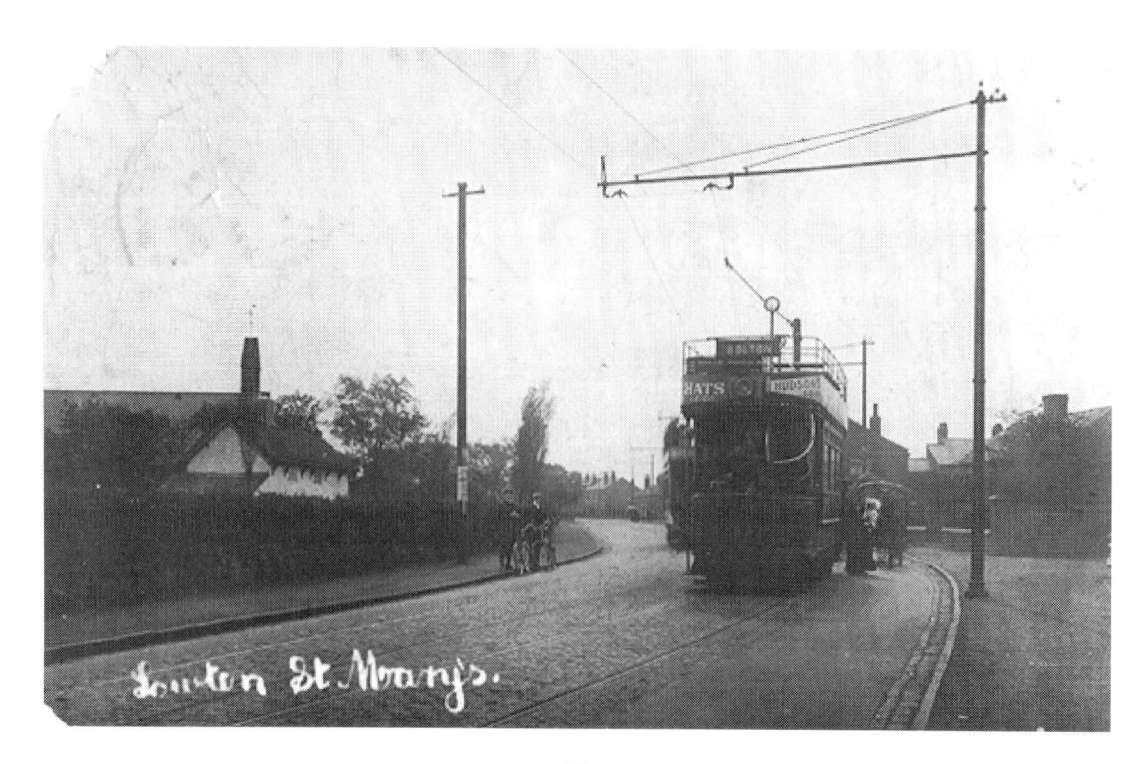

Above-
Victoria Ballroom was over Flints shop where dances were held every Saturday in the 1920's and 1930's.

Knotts mill is in the distance.

Below-
Across the road from Flints was Ruffley's bakery and fleet of delivery vans.

Photo courtesy of Wigan M.B.C.

Above-
Formerly the building on this site was used as a Sunday School and Anglican services were held there. When St. Marys was built in 1860 the premises became the Church inn. It is thought that the Millstone Inn across the road transferred the licence to the new inn. The Millstone was dated 1620.

Below-
Another view of Newton Road with a very old house by the Church and the Leigh Friendly Society Co-op shop near left.

Photo courtesy of Wigan M.B.C.
Above-
Shepherds Inn on the Leigh and Lowton boundary almost as well known by the last generation as "Th' owd Terminus". Originally the trams only ran to the Leigh boundary.

Below-
Washend Farm now a housing estate.

81

Above-
Cottages on Newton Road near the Leigh boundary.

Below-
Clay Hill Farm on Canaan, a group of houses on the Leigh - Lowton boundary.

Above-
At one time a small holding on Canaan

Below-
A few of the ten or so cottages on Canaan all of which have been modernised.

Above- Lowton Hall Farm.
This very large old house was demolished in the 1930's. In 18th Century it was farmed by a Mr. Leigh who was also running a tannery business on the premises. His fortune was left to Mary Leigh who helped to build St. Marys Church and School. The last occupant of the hall was Mr. Thomas Leigh the hay and straw dealer. His family still carry on that business from Pocket Nook Farm.

Right-
At one time the Marsh family shown here occupied part of the hall. The entrance to the drive of the hall was almost opposite Hesketh Meadow Lane. The drive also led to several cottages to the left and behind the hall. The little group was called Penkethman Fold.

Left-
Mather Cottage only demolished in the middle of this century. In the 16th Century the Mather family lived there, one of their sons Richard born in 1596 was to become famous as a preacher, but was accused of heresy. In 1635 he sailed to America since then that family have gained "honour and renown throughout the world". Richard Richyard's memories of Lowton relates this story.

Photo courtesy of Wigan M.B.C.

Below-
One of the last steam trains in St. Marys station.

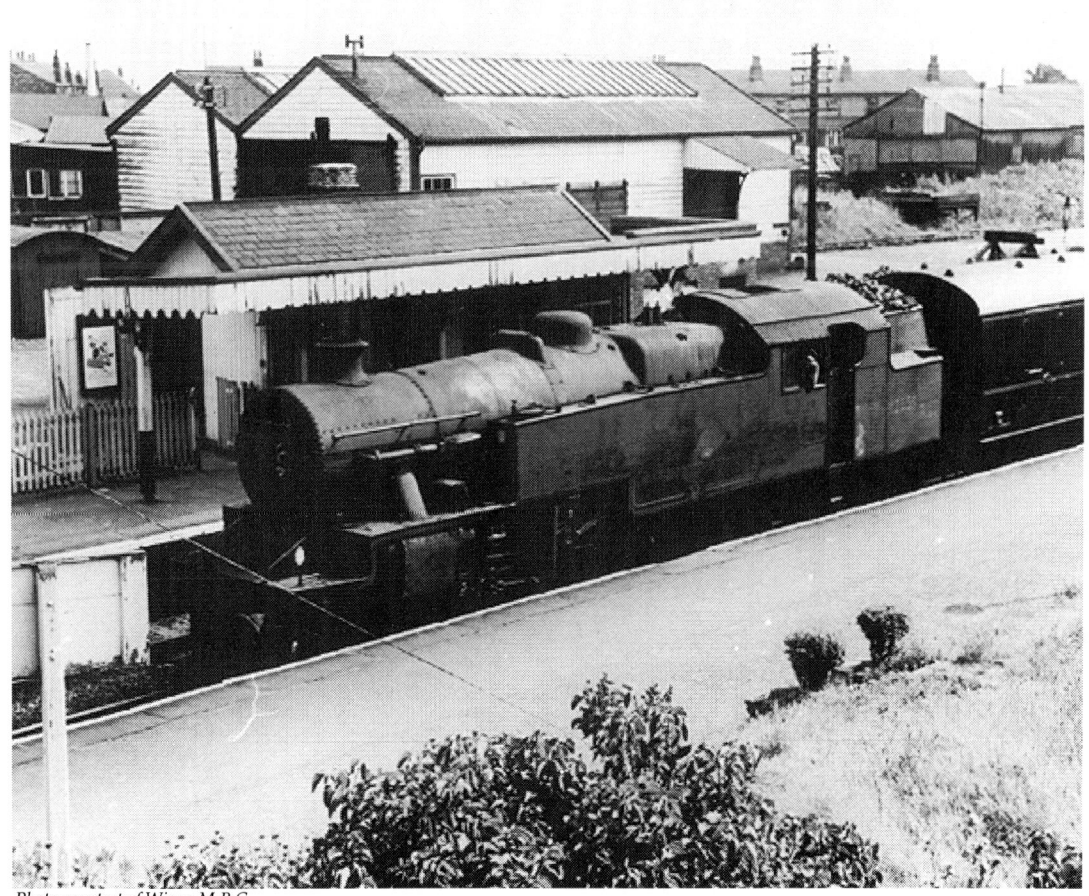

Photo courtest of Wigan M.B.C.

85

Above- St. Marys Station.
Note the covered foot bridge which was entered directly off the middle of the road bridge.

Below-
Showing the water tank and booking office, beyond are the warehouses and goods yard.

Above- Fairy House Farm.
The best example of an old farmhouse in the area. As far as can be ascertained it was built in 1586, the foundations are sandstone blocks, and the oak timbers in the walls can still be seen. There are two large ingle nook fire places, and in one gable end there are four or five oak mullion windows.
In the picture is Mr. Landers and his family about 1880.

Above and left-
Higher Pocket Nook Farm and attached out buildings. Occupied by Mr. E. Leigh who was born at Lowton Hall. The family still run the hay and straw business.

Right- 156 Newton Road.
A typical weavers cottage, picture taken in 1929 of Mrs Margaret Taylor and her grandson. Mrs. Taylor finished weaving in 1900, her granddaughter still has samples of her work. This cottage had a one loom "shop". Two doors away at 160, there was a two loom shop. Shop was the local word for weaving room.

Below- Gregorys Row.
There were three rows of cottages similar to this, Hayes and Inces, all were weavers cottages. At the farther end of this row was a small factory weaving shed.

Above-
Bond Street in the 1940's.

Below-
Very old cottages in Brook Street all of which have been modernised

Above- Red House Farm.
Another of the farms built on the common later to become Unsworths Nurseries.

Below-
These cottages were once again just a cottage with farm buildings attached, animals were kept here within living memory. There were several acres of land to the holding.

Left-
Green House Farm on Shuttle Street, off Sandy Lane. Two generations ago people referred to the Lane as "Goo'ing down't Shuttle".

Sadly there are no pictures of the house, but the views of the old barn are worth preserving.

The front view shows the date of 1616, while the back view shows the old barn door opening on to the Threshing floor.

Photographs taken 1957.

Right-
Brook House an Eighteenth Century small holding on the Lowton - Pennington boundary. The design of the house is typical of many built at that period. Highfield Farm on the other side of the village is a good example.

Below-
Liptrot Cottage and barn close by Brook House, the lane leading to both properties and Liptrot Farm was known as "Gooin' down't Gravel".

Above- Liptrot Farm.
Occupied in the early part of the century by Messrs E. and J. Howarth who were the first to own a pedigree herd of Friesian cattle in the village. It is said the cows were never turned out but fed freshly mown grass everyday in spring and summer from tthe flood meadows on the farm.
For many years now Mr. Henery Whittle and his family have farmed there.

Below-
 Mr. Allan Grundy took over the farm after the Howarths, here he is with his work man Mr. Frank Walmesley and two of his prize winning animals.

Above- Carr Farm.
On the Lowton - Kenyon boundary occupied at the turn of the century by Joseph and Emma Arnold pictured here. It is now farmed by the Adamson family.

Below-
Pocket Nook Farm another farm on the boundary, house and buildings under one roof. Both farms were once part of Earl Wiltons estate.

An aerial view of the properties that were once Joseph Leigh's nurseries. At the turn of the century Mr. Leigh began his business from the old cottage in the foreground, later he was able to build three fine houses for himself and for each of his two sons. The houses are built of the "best Ruabon brick" and are a measure of the success he acheived. Mr. Leigh made his fortune growing pot plants and specialising in tulip growing. A railway siding was provided for him at St. Marys station to transport his produce to his stall on Smithfield Market, Manchester. Mr. Leigh's foreman Mr. Marsh later lived in the old cottage and eventually became the owner of the business. One of the houses was demolished some time ago, and recently the cottage was also taken down

Left-
One of the three houses built by Joseph Leigh on Sandy Lane.

Above-
Laburnum Farm on Slag Lane, Eighteenth Century.

Below-
Although Gilded Hollins Farm is in Pennington it played a significant part in the developement of Methodism in Lowton.

Above-
Mr. Taylor the baker on Golborne Dale Road by the Richard Evans Coal Wharf near the Bulls Head.

Below-
A charabanc outing in the early Twenties. The Hare and Hounds in the back ground.

Right-
Mr. Jack Worsley who for many years ran a taxi service fron Newton-le-Willows Station.

Below-
Mrs. Hayes the local midwife retired in the 1930's after serving the village for 50 years.
Her contemporaries were Mrs. Adamson and Mrs Murphy.

Below-
Matt Howarth one of the two Lowton Blacksmiths. A well known character, he kept two sets of boxing gloves in the smithy so that the local youths could settle their differences under the Marquess of Queensberry Rules.

Above-
Girl Guides 1950's.

Below-
Boys Brigade Band.

Photo courtesy of Wigan M.B.C.

Above-
A production of "The Magic Key" by Lane Head Methodists about 1950.

Below-
Jim Farrington and Walter Mort near Manor Farm after the heavy snow fall of 28th January 1940.

Golborne District Chairman Albert Brown handing over the room at the Meadows to the scouts.

Lowton St. Marys Scout troop was founded by Alec Hughes in 1961 meeting in the old school. As the numbers of pupils increased at the school, the Scouts had to move to a room at the Meadows then as vandalism drove them from the Meadows the Vicar Rev. Newby let them use the old vicarage stables, with the arrival of a new vicar the troop moved back to the new school then in 1980 money was raised to build the present headquarters at the school. At this time Alec Hughes left Lowton Scouts to take appointment as Assistant District Commissioner in the Leigh district.

In 1962 the Lowton Scouts built a pedal car to enter in the Scouts Soapbox Derby, these are races for cars built by scouts under 14 years old using parts of old cycles, pram wheels etc. the races are a national event held north, south, east & west at Blackpool, Brighton, Cleethorpes & Plymouth and Lowton have had considerable success over the years, in 1970 Alec Hughes was invited to join the organising committee for the national races, meeting at scout headquarters in London and is still a member.

In April 1982 Alec Hughes was awarded the second highest award in the Scouts, The Silver Acorn, in recognition of 'specially distinguished service'.

"Skip" Alec Hughes.
Taken at the races in Brighton in 1980. The car is called "Sparrow" in recognition of the local nickname "Lowton Sparrows". Mr. Stuart Walwyn is the present Group Scout Leader.

Right- Mother's Union Concert (about 1964).

Scouts and Cubs from the 1st Lowton St. Mary's troop also taking part.

Right-
Lowton St. Marys Cub Scout team after winning the Leigh District football cup in its inauguration year 1969.

Right-
Lowton Youth Club football team 1946.

Above-
Lowton St. Mary's Church Council taken at the Centenery November 1961. Seated the vicar Rev. Newby and his wife with Alec Hughes the vicar's warden on his right. On his left the Peoples warden R. Harrison and Treasurer R. Howarth.
Below-
230th Birthday Celebrations at St. Lukes.

Right- St. Lukes School.
Mrs. Chadwick and Tom Wood with class circa 1930

Right-
Headmaster Tom Wood with class circa 1934.

Right-
Mrs. Barnes and Tom Wood with class circa 1935.

Above-
Headmaster Mr. Thomas Barnes and Standard 3 + 4 in 1913.

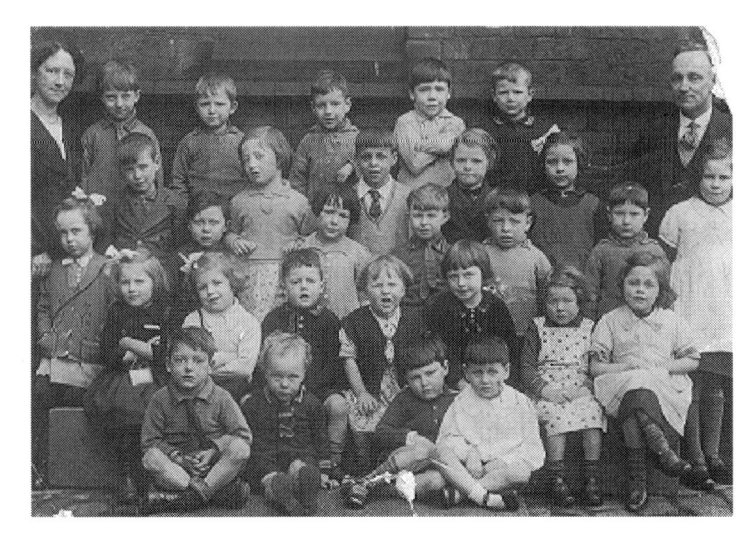

Left-
Scholars at St.Marys Church School Early 1920's.

Left-
A class from the "Chapel School" with Mr. Vaudrey the headmaster and Mrs. Gregory. Note the little girls wearing clogs.

Photo courtesy of Wigan M.B.C.

Above-
Sailors of H.M.S. Gosling stationed at Hesketh Meadow taking part in the Rose Queen procession for St. Mary's Church.

Right-
The camp was later taken over by the Americans who built this cinema, which is now Lowton Civic Hall.

Above-
Peter Kane serving his apprenticeship at the smithy, Kenyon Lane, Lane Head, seen here striking for Chris Jordon the blacksmith. In the background is son Bert Jordan who ran the business until recently, the family were smiths for over 60 years.

Left-
Peter Kane became fly weight champion of the world in 1938. He had a wonderful record winning 87 fights losing only 7.

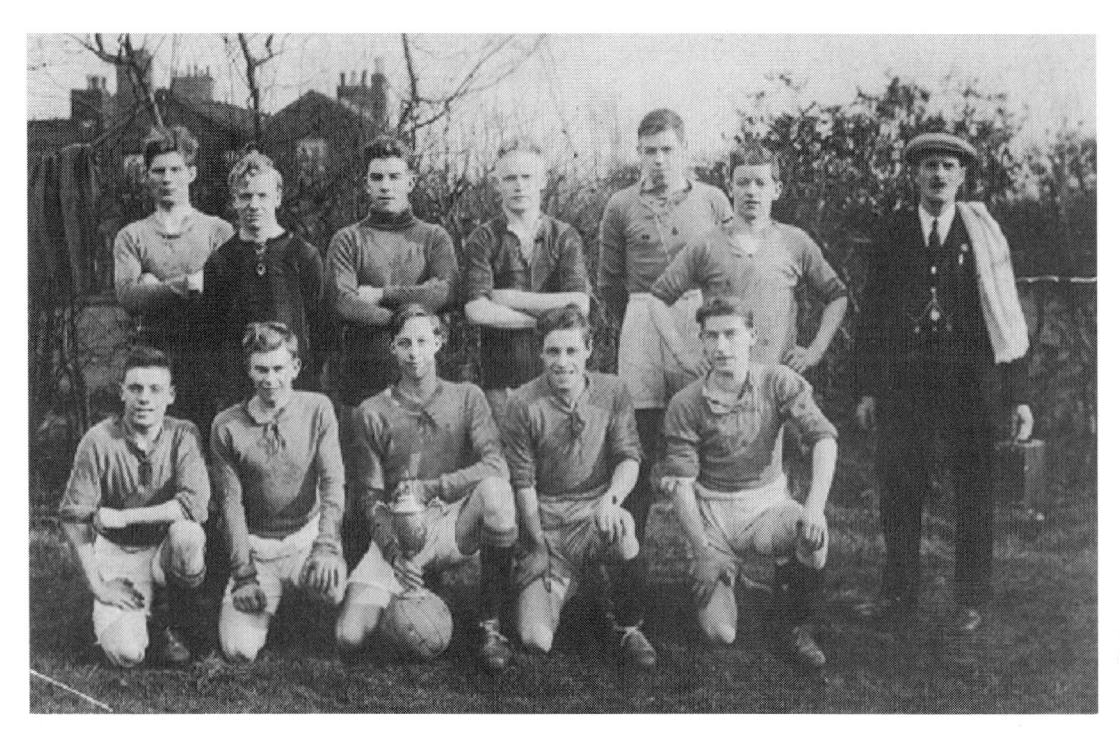

Above- Lowton Football Team 1920's.
Back L to R - J. Russell, J. Hatton, W. Russell, N. Johnson, C. Ball, J. Battersby.
Front L to R - J. Williams, M. Smallman, W. Turton, E. Price, J. Price, T. Price (Trainer).

Right-
Harold Eckersley of Lowton with his trainer Mr. W.C. Hughes and the trophy for the International Cross Country Championship which he won at Ayr, Scotland in 1928.

He was selected for the International C.C.C, in 1925, 1928, 1930. Winner of 14 first prizes, 10 seconds, and 9 thirds.

Above-
Lancashire County Cricket Team. County Champions 1930.
Back Row L to R - G. Duckworth, J. L. Hopwood, J. Iddon, F. M. Sibbles, G. Honeson, M. L.Taylor, E. Paynter.
Front Row L to R - C. Hallows, E. Tyldesley, P. T. Ecckersley (capt), E. D. Mc Donald, R. Tyldeslet.

Peter Thorpe Eckersley was born at Lime House Lowton in 1904, he played for Lancashire C.C. as an amateur from 1923 to 1935 being captain from 1929 to 1935.

He was also a keen amateur pilot, landing his plane many times on Mr. Rigbys field at Locking Stoops Farm. One unique record was that he arranged the first flight ever to take a cricket team to a fixture. Two planes were used to take the Lancashire team from Cardiff to Southhampton. The journey took 51 minutes.

He also became M.P. for Manchester Exchange Division in 1935. At the out break of war in 1939 he immediatly joined the Air Arm of the R.N.V.R although he could have claimed exemption on the grounds of being M.P. He was killed less than a year later.

George Duckworth also had family connections with Lowton, his mother being one of the Watsons in Church Lane.

Above- Moss Pit.
A sandy bottomed pond were over the years thousands have bathed. This seems to be a Sunday School outing on Highfield Moss around 1900.

Below-
Highfield Moss used as a firing range by the Prince of Wales volunteers from 1870 - 1908. The target was on the bank in the distance, the picture taken from one of the firing butts, two more can be seen at intervals of about 100 yards.

Above-
Prisoners of War hay making at Highfield Farm 1948.

Below-
Plane crash at Highfield in the early 1930's. The plane was from an Air Circus using Mr. Rigby's field at Locking Stoops Farm. The pilot and two paying passengers escaped unhurt in the picture are Miss. Bridge, Harold Laybourne, Les Worsley, H. Worsley, Stan Porter, J. W. Worsley, Miss. B. Miller and her sister Pauline.

Two pictures of the Millingford brook on the Lowton - Golborne boundary.